U.S. STATE FLOWERS IN COUNTED CROSS-STITCH

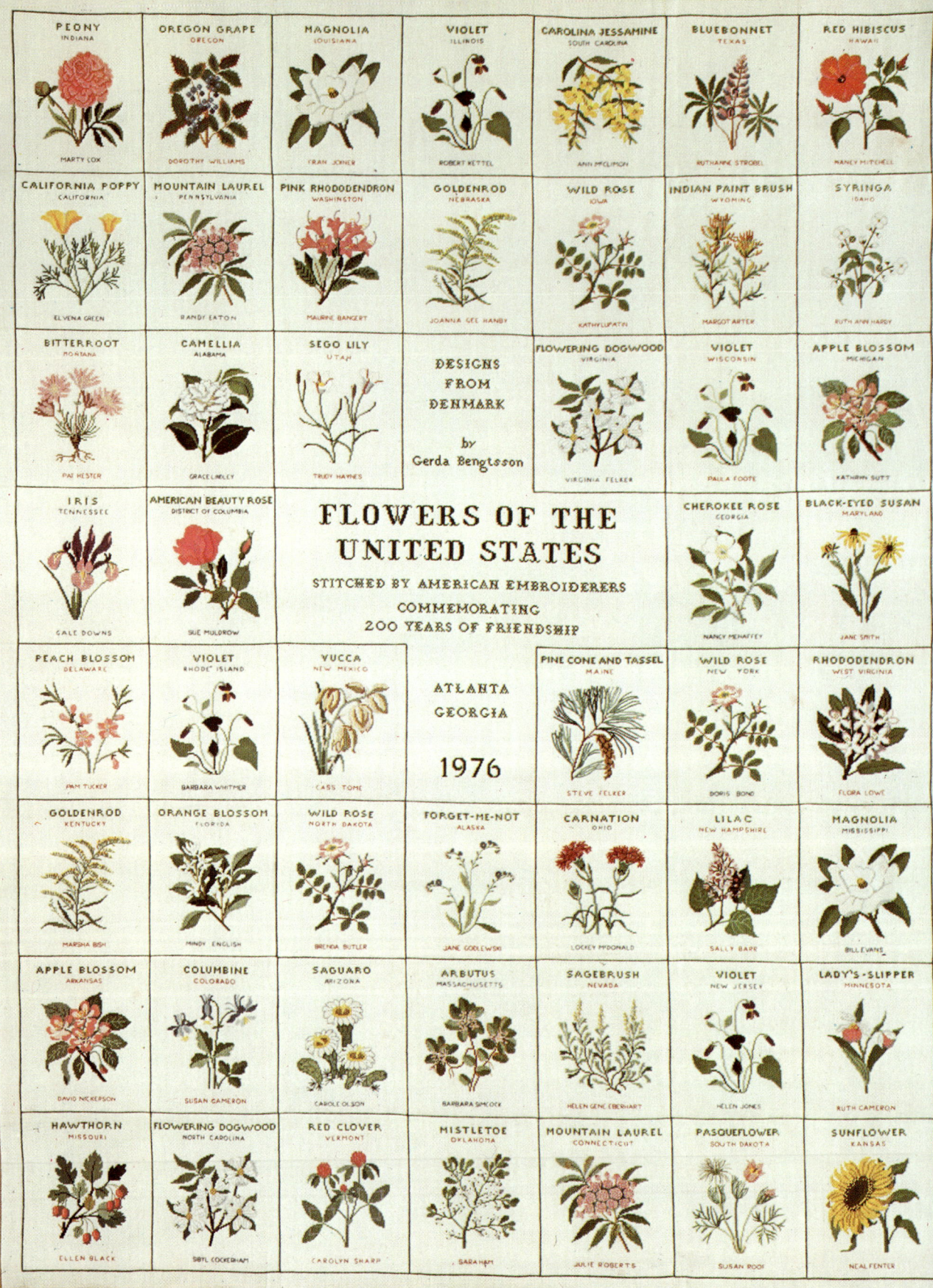

U.S. STATE FLOWERS IN COUNTED CROSS-STITCH

**Gerda Bengtsson
and
The Danish Handcraft Guild
with Ginnie Thompson**

Diagrams prepared by Judie Schaal

VAN NOSTRAND REINHOLD COMPANY
New York Cincinnati Toronto London Melbourne

Front cover and Frontispiece:
Wall hanging of the fifty-one flowers of the United States designed by Gerda Bengtsson and stitched by American embroiderers to commemorate the Bicentennial and acknowledge the long friendship between Denmark and the United States. It measures 44 by 58 inches and is worked with Danish Flower Thread on 34-threads-to-the-inch linen in colors specified by Gerda Bengtsson. Reproduced courtesy of Felker Art-Needlework, Inc., 640 Valley Brook Road, Decatur, Georgia 30033. Photo, Malcolm Varon, New York.

Photographs on pages 10, 11, and 12 reproduced courtesy The Hammock Shop, Pawleys Island, South Carolina 29585.

Library of Congress Catalog Card Number 76-16681
ISBN 0-442-20683-6

All rights reserved.
No part of this work may be reproduced or used in any form or by any means—graphic, electronic, or mechanical, including photocopying, recording, or information storage and retrieval systems—without written permission of the publisher.
Printed in the United States of America.

Published in 1977 by Van Nostrand Reinhold Company Inc.
135 West 50th Street, New York, NY 10020, USA

Fleet Publishers
1410 Birchmount Road,
Scarborough, Ontario M1P 2E7, Canada

Van Nostrand Reinhold Australia Pty. Limited
480 Latrobe Street, Victoria 3000, Australia

Van Nostrand Reinhold Company Limited
Molly Millars Lane, Wokingham, Berkshire RG11 2PY, England

16 15 14 13 12 11 10 9 8 7 6 5 4 3

Library of Congress Cataloging in Publication Data
Bengtsson, Gerda.
   U. S. State flowers in counted cross-stitch.

   Includes index.
   1. Cross-stitch—Patterns. 2. State flowers.
I. Thompson, Ginnie, joint author. II. Danish Handcraft Guild. III. Title.
TT778.C76B47   746.4′4   76-16681
ISBN 0-442-20683-6

TABLE OF CONTENTS

Preface   6
Materials   7
Method of Working   8
Examples of Finished Designs   10
The State Flowers: Diagrams and Illustrations   13
   Alabama (Camellia)   14
   Alaska (Forget-Me-Not)   16
   Arizona (Saguaro)   18
   Arkansas (Apple Blossom)   20
   California (California Poppy)   22
   Colorado (Columbine)   24
   Connecticut (Mountain Laurel)   26
   Delaware (Peach Blossom)   28
   District of Columbia (American Beauty Rose)   30
   Florida (Orange Blossom)   32
   Georgia (Cherokee Rose)   34
   Hawaii (Red Hibiscus)   36
   Idaho (Syringa)   38
   Illinois (Violet)   40
   Indiana (Peony)   42
   Iowa (Wild Rose)   68
   Kansas (Sunflower)   44
   Kentucky (Goldenrod)   46
   Louisiana (Magnolia)   48
   Maine (Pine Cone and Tassel)   50
   Maryland (Black-Eyed Susan)   52
   Massachusetts (Arbutus)   54
   Michigan (Apple Blossom)   20
   Minnesota (Lady's Slipper)   56
   Mississippi (Magnolia)   48
   Missouri (Hawthorn)   58
   Montana (Bitterroot)   60
   Nebraska (Goldenrod)   46
   Nevada (Sagebrush)   62
   New Hampshire (Lilac)   64
   New Jersey (Violet)   40
   New Mexico (Yucca)   66
   New York (Wild Rose)   68
   North Carolina (Flowering Dogwood)   70
   North Dakota (Wild Rose)   68
   Ohio (Carnation)   72
   Oklahoma (Mistletoe)   74
   Oregon (Oregon Grape)   76
   Pennsylvania (Mountain Laurel)   26
   Rhode Island (Violet)   40
   South Carolina (Carolina Jessamine)   78
   South Dakota (Pasqueflower)   80
   Tennessee (Iris)   82
   Texas (Bluebonnet)   84
   Utah (Sego Lily)   86
   Vermont (Red Clover)   88
   Virginia (Flowering Dogwood)   70
   Washington (Pink Rhododendron)   90
   West Virginia (Rhododendron)   92
   Wisconsin (Violet)   40
   Wyoming (Indian Paint Brush)   94
Suppliers   96
Index   96

PREFACE

Counted cross-stitch samplers are a beloved part of our American heritage. In this bicentennial year, it is unexpected but appropriate to have a pattern book of the state flowers of the United States that was designed by a Dane. It is fitting because the Danes have been the primary reason for the revival of cross-stitch—an art form we consider American—in this country and the world. Cross-stitch, however, did not originate here. It is an ancient art. Gerda Bengtsson, chief designer of the Danish Handcraft Guild, more than any other individual is responsible for the revival of counted cross-stitch embroidery today.

Some years ago, an American Army major on leave in Denmark became enthralled with the artistry of Danish needlework and suggested to Gerda Bengtsson that the beauty of the flower of each State of the Union be rendered in the exquisite embroidery of the Guild. In 1961 Gerda Bengtsson undertook the difficult job of designing these flowers in cross-stitch. First she had to collect the flowers—for she will work only from the living plant, observing the flower in all its stages of growth. Although she had descriptive material in her botanical library, she had none of the blossoms in her private herbarium. The Danish Botanical Gardens yielded some twenty plants. Other specimens were obtained from the Admiral of the Danish Navy who is an amateur botanist, her postman, butcher, and many others. The few that could not be found in all of Denmark were sent by air freight from friendly Americans overseas.

The work of collecting, studying, painting the living flowers, transferring their images to the drawing board, and finally recreating them in the delicate Danish needlework took three years. They are reproduced here in all their beauty so you too can have the pleasure of stitching them.

—Ginnie Thompson

MATERIALS

NEEDLE AND THREAD

It is essential to use a small, blunt tapestry needle, size 24, 25, or 26 for cross-stitch. The embroidery thread originally used for these designs is Danish Flower Thread. This is a mat-finished, thicker thread, one strand equalling two strands of DMC 6-strand-mercerized-cotton embroidery floss. It is especially dyed by Ejnar Hansen of synthetic dyes that closely approximate vegetable dyes. Danish Flower Thread has a magic quality but special care in laundering is advised.

DMC embroidery floss may be preferred as being more readily available. Two of the six strands work well on most of the evenweave linens suggested.

FABRIC

Evenweave linen is the almost exclusive preference of the Danish Handcraft Guild but Americans, lacking a rigid tradition, use evenweave cottons, wools, and blends. On pages 10 and 11 are a wastebasket of burlap and an afghan of a polyacrylic fabric that resembles wool in appearance. The wastebasket was stitched with 4 DMC threads; the afghan, with 2 Danish Flower Threads or 3 threads of DMC floss. For the state flower designs either evenweave linen 30 threads per inch or a coarser evenweave linen 18 threads per inch is recommended.

STITCHFINDER

An accessory finding favor in the United States and Europe is a Stitchfinder ©—a metal sheet with two strip magnets. The metal sheet slips behind the design chart (even one bound in a book). The magnetic strips are used on top of the chart to mark the exact line of stitching or to bracket the area being worked.

METHOD OF WORKING

There are two excellent techniques for doing counted cross-stitch. The traditional European method employs a sewing-stitch motion with the fabric held over the index finger. The American method uses a small embroidery hoop and the stab-stitch as recommended by the late Rose Wilder Lane, foremost American needlewoman. While the European technique is speedier, the American technique employing the hoop offers more control, just as a frame does for needlepoint. Either technique may be used for the designs in this book.

The stab-stitch method requires a 4-inch, 5-inch, or 6-inch screw-type hoop on which the fabric is kept taut. (Any slight distortion of the fabric can be corrected by "raking" the weave with a needle.) The stab-stitch employs two separate motions—one up and one down.

LINEN STITCHERY TECHNIQUES

In 1930, when I first started to draw plant motifs for cross-stitching, I used a very simple technique. It had its own charm, but the drawback was that many of my patterns produced in this way were botanically incorrect. By developing a new technique, however, which employed not only whole cross-stitches but backstitches, cross-stitches shifted over by a thread, and half cross-stitches when necessary, they came to resemble the plants more. For big plants with simple shapes, however, or when working on canvas, I still use the whole cross-stitch by itself.

A. Sew cross-stitch from left to right. Sew all the under-stitches first. Each under-stitch goes diagonally over two threads from the bottom left corner to the top right. Sew the over-stitches on the way back, to finish the cross.

B. Cross-stitch sewn downwards. Finish each stitch before going on to the next, making sure that the over-stitch lies in the same direction as in diagram A.

The wrong side of A and B should look like vertical stitching only.

C. Staggered cross-stitches.

D. Two different versions of backstitch lines. On the left the top stitch goes two threads to the side and two threads down; the bottom stitch passes over two threads horizontally. On the right the top stitch passes over two threads downwards but only one thread to the side, and the fourth stitch goes two threads to the side and one thread down. There are also one vertical stitch and one horizontal stitch.

E. Four backstitches, two sewn over one thread and two sewn over one intersection of two threads.

F. On the left are four three-quarter cross-stitches. On the right are half cross-stitches, which cover only one thread in one direction and two threads in the other.

On fabric where each cross-stitch is done over one thread rather than two, compensating stitches are used in place of split stitches. The split stitch is either omitted or used as a complete cross-stitch.

HEM STITCH

The hem stitch is a particular kind of stitch needed for hemming, with or without the use of drawn threads. Naturally, it is worked on the reverse side of the pattern. In A, the needle passes under a group of threads from right to left. Then, in B, one small stitch is made down into the hem just to the right of the threads previously encircled.

DETERMINING THE SIZE OF A PROJECT

The technique for cross-stitching on linen requires crossing 2 threads horizontally and 2 threads vertically for each square on the design chart. Thus linen with a count of 30 threads per inch will use 15 stitches per inch; linen that is 27 threads per inch will use approximately 18 stitches per inch; 18 threads will be 9 stitches per inch; etc. To work the flower designs as a picture including the state name, flower name, and cross-stitch border, the following procedure would be used to determine the fabric requirements:

1. Count the number of squares across the width and height of the design between the cross-stitched borders. (Notice that the charts are marked off in tens by a heavier line for ease in counting.)
2. Divide each of these numbers by the number of stitches per inch in the fabric you have chosen to use.
3. Add an allowance for a border all around and an allowance to turn under for a hem.

It is preferable to cut your fabric too large and waste a little, than to spend time and effort stitching on too small a piece and be disappointed with the results.

WASHING AND IRONING INSTRUCTIONS

Danish Flower Thread is dyed with the best and truest dyes that can be manufactured. The colored threads, however, often contain an excess of dye, which bleeds in washing. It is important, therefore, that those who use the Danish Flower Thread follow exactly the instructions for washing and ironing given below.

Washing. The embroidery must be rinsed several times in cold water, thereafter washed by hand in cold or lukewarm water with soap flakes (not powder), rinsed again in cold water several times, and then squeezed carefully and laid to dry between 2 white cloths.

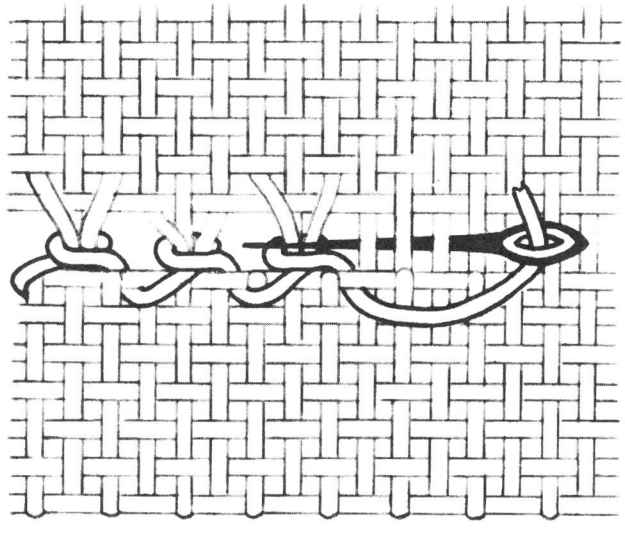

A

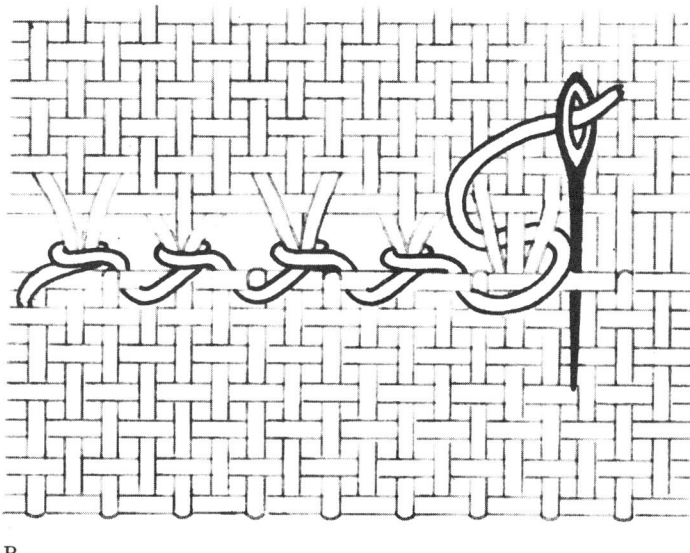

B

Ironing. Never sprinkle the embroidery with water or roll it up; it must be laid with the right side down on a soft under-cloth. Place a piece of wrung-out gauze or some other thin material on top of it and iron until the material is dry. Then iron directly on the reverse side of the embroidery until it is quite dry.

MOUNTING

To mount a picture, lace the finished, pressed embroidery onto a good quality white matboard using button and carpet thread. Do not use glue. If a glass-fronted frame is desired, non-glare glass is recommended by the Guild.

Afghan by Joy King and Mabel Fitzpatrick.

Album cover, stitcher not known; handbag insert by Lynn Miller, wastebasket by Judie Schaal.

THE STATE FLOWERS: DIAGRAMS AND ILLUSTRATIONS

Every tenth line on the diagrams for the state flower designs is done in a heavier line for ease in counting stitches. Some states have the same state flower. In these cases, more than one state name is given on the diagram.

Under the diagram for each design is a chart that gives the symbols for the stitches and colors of threads to be used. Backstitch symbols are given first, then the symbols for cross-stitch variations—short squat stitches or tall skinny stitches—and finally the symbol for the basic cross-stitch. To the right of the stitch symbols are given the DMC embroidery floss (DMC) color number and the corresponding Danish Flower Thread (DFT) color number, and the color name.

Framed pictures by Jesselyn Riggsbee; box cover, stitcher not known; tray inserts by Virginia Gerlinger and Linda Webster.

CAMELLIA
ALABAMA

DMC	DFT		DMC	DFT		DMC	DFT
3023	7		500	210		White	
Lt. beige			Deep dk. green				
452	19		320	10		928	35
Med. gray			Med. green			Lt. gray	
834	47		471	40		610	215
Lt. gold-green			Lt. green			Brown	
987	100		792	228			
Dk. green			Dk. gray blue				

CAMELLIA

ALABAMA

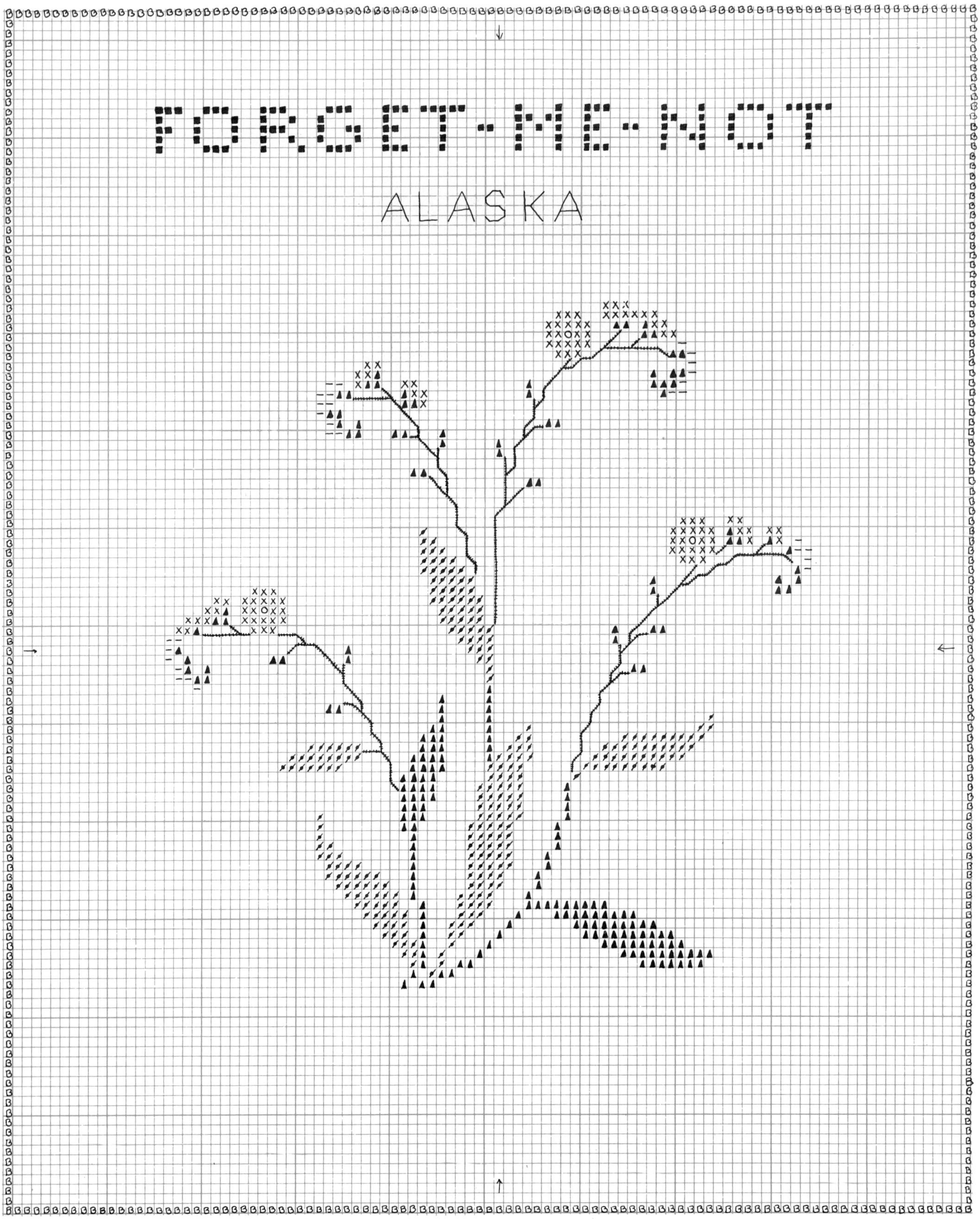

FORGET-ME-NOT
ALASKA

DMC	DFT		DMC	DFT
225		Soft pink	798	22	Med. blue
743	48	Bright yellow	987	100	Dk. green
3053	223	Lt. soft green	792	228	Dk. gray blue
320	10	Med. green	610	215	Brown

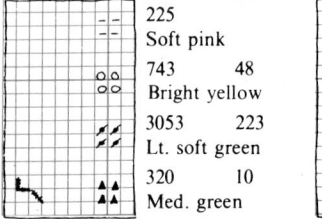
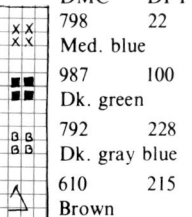

FORGET-ME-NOT
ALASKA

SAGUARO
ARIZONA

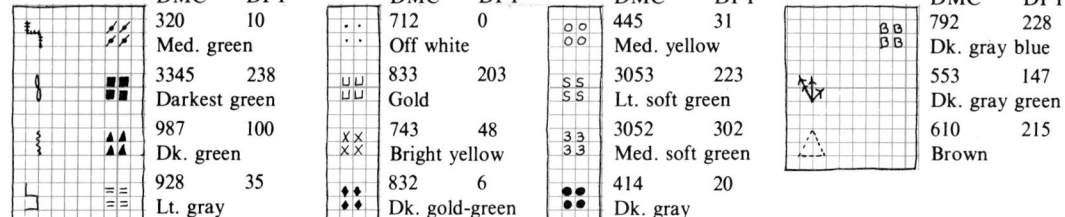

	DMC	DFT		DMC	DFT		DMC	DFT		DMC	DFT
	320	10	· ·	712	0	o o	445	31	B B	792	228
	Med. green			Off white			Med. yellow			Dk. gray blue	
■ ■	3345	238	U U	833	203	S S	3053	223		553	147
	Darkest green			Gold			Lt. soft green			Dk. gray green	
▲ ▲	987	100	X X	743	48	3 3	3052	302		610	215
	Dk. green			Bright yellow			Med. soft green			Brown	
= =	928	35	♦ ♦	832	6	● ●	414	20			
	Lt. gray			Dk. gold-green			Dk. gray				

APPLE BLOSSOM

ARKANSAS

MICHIGAN

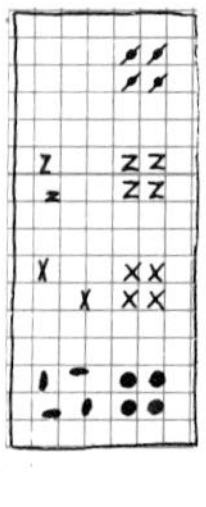

DMC	DFT		DMC	DFT		DMC	DFT		DMC	DFT
320	10		3345	238		600	88		792	228
Med. green			Darkest green			Med. red			Dk. gray blue	
3053	223		838	216		899 + 758 (mixed DMC)			610	215
Lt. soft green			Deep dk. brown			Dk. pink			Brown	
3052	302		734	26		353				
Med. soft green			Med. gold-green			Med. pink				
987	100		743	48		754				
Dk. green			Bright yellow			Lt. pink				

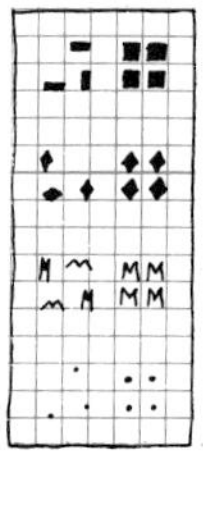

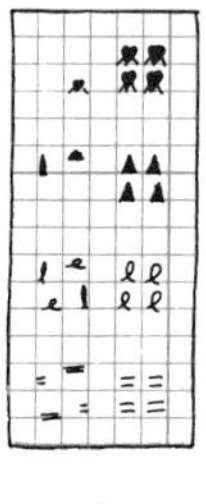

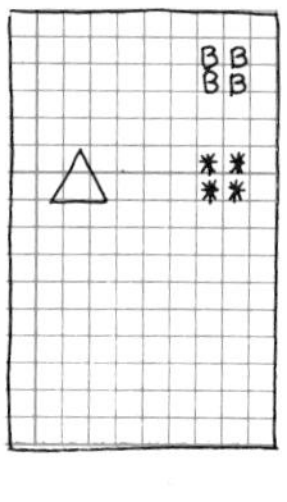

APPLE BLOSSOM
ARKANSAS

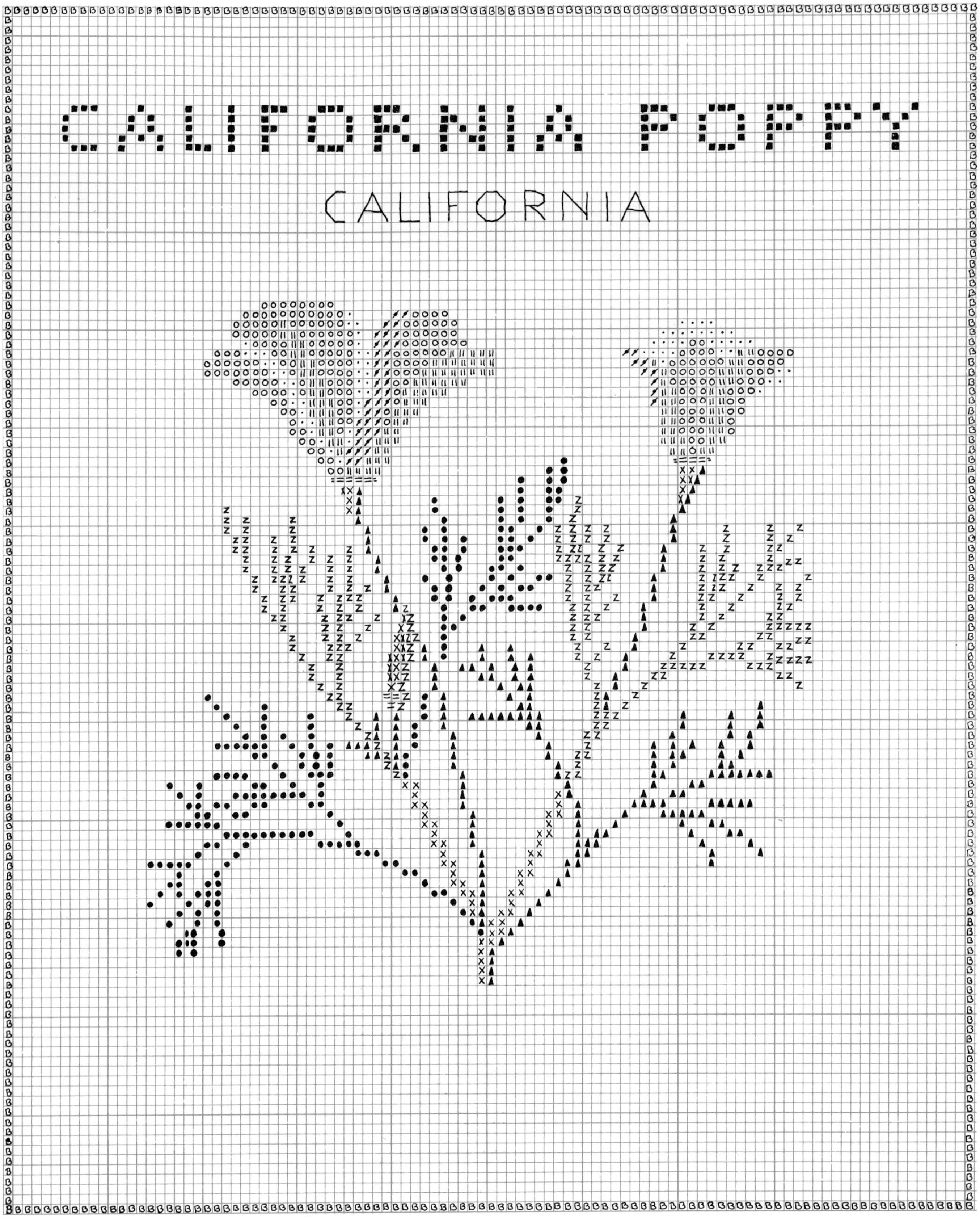

CALIFORNIA POPPY
CALIFORNIA

DMC	DFT	
445	31	Med. yellow
743	48	Bright yellow
977	54	Rust
834	47	Lt. gold-green
677	225	Lt. gold
471	40	Lt. green
910	8	Bright green
320	10	Med. green
986	9	Med. dk. green
987	100	Dk. green
792	228	Dk. gray blue
610	215	Brown

COLUMBINE
COLORADO

	DMC	DFT
	932	229
		Lt. gray blue
	322	227
		Med. gray blue
	928	35
		Lt. gray
	712	0
		Off white

	DMC	DFT
	3053	223
		Lt. soft green
	320	10
		Med. green
	987	100
		Dk. green
	3345	238
		Darkest green

	DMC	DFT
	743	48
		Bright yellow
	792	228
		Dk. gray blue
	610	215
		Brown

COLUMBINE
COLORADO

MOUNTAIN LAUREL

CONNECTICUT

PENNSYLVANIA

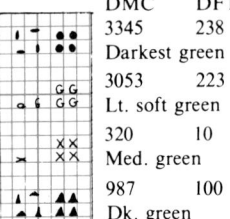
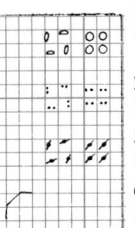

DMC	DFT	
3345	238	Darkest green
3053	223	Lt. soft green
320	10	Med. green
987	100	Dk. green
3354	3	Lt. dusty pink
	225	Lt. pink
3350	205	Dk. pink
610	215	Brown
734	26	Med. gold-green
832	6	Dk. gold-green
792	228	Dk. gray blue

MOUNTAIN LAUREL
CONNECTICUT

PEACH BLOSSOM
DELAWARE

DMC	DFT		DMC	DFT		DMC	DFT	
471	40	Lt. green	902	4	Dk. burgundy	776	69	Lt. pink
320	10	Med. green	743	48	Bright yellow	962	2	Med. dusty pink
732	34	Olive green	3052	302	Med. soft green	3042	27	Lt. gray violet
987	100	Dk. green	792	228	Dk. gray blue	610	215	Brown

AMERICAN BEAUTY ROSE
DISTRICT OF COLUMBIA

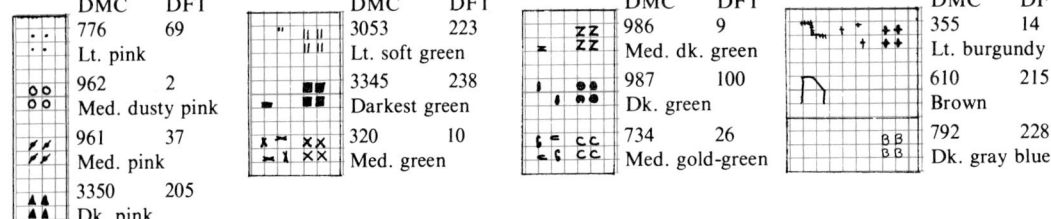

DMC	DFT		DMC	DFT		DMC	DFT		DMC	DFT
776	69		3053	223		986	9		355	14
Lt. pink			Lt. soft green			Med. dk. green			Lt. burgundy	
962	2		3345	238		987	100		610	215
Med. dusty pink			Darkest green			Dk. green			Brown	
961	37		320	10		734	26		792	228
Med. pink			Med. green			Med. gold-green			Dk. gray blue	
3350	205									
Dk. pink										

AMERICAN BEAUTY ROSE
DISTRICT OF COLUMBIA

ORANGE BLOSSOM
FLORIDA

CHEROKEE ROSE
GEORGIA

DMC	DFT		DMC	DFT		DMC	DFT
743	48		320	10		3052	302
Bright yellow			Med. green			Med. soft green	
White			987	100		3053	223
			Dk. green			Lt. soft green	
833	203		3345	238		3023	7
Gold			Darkest green			Lt. beige	
223	15		792	228		610	215
Grayish red			Dk. gray blue			Brown	

34

RED HIBISCUS
HAWAII

DMC	DFT		DMC	DFT		DMC	DFT
891	86		776	69		987	100
Lt. red			Lt. pink			Dk. green	
3685	411		962	2		3345	238
Med. burgundy			Med. dusty pink			Darkest green	
902	4		988	101		792	228
Dk. burgundy			Bright yellow-green			Dk. gray blue	
743	48		320	10		610	215
Bright yellow			Med. green			Brown	

RED HIBISCUS

HAWAII

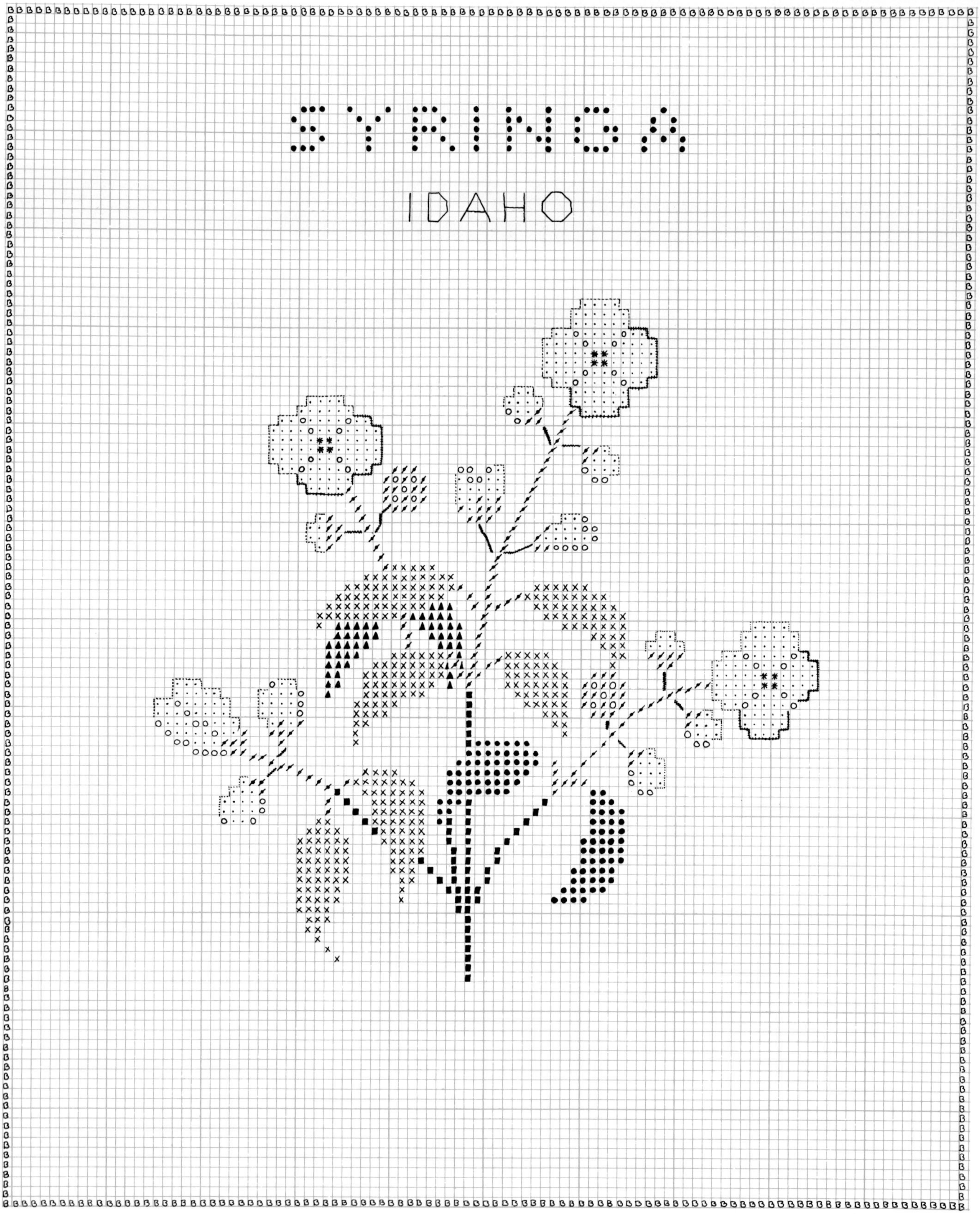

SYRINGA
IDAHO

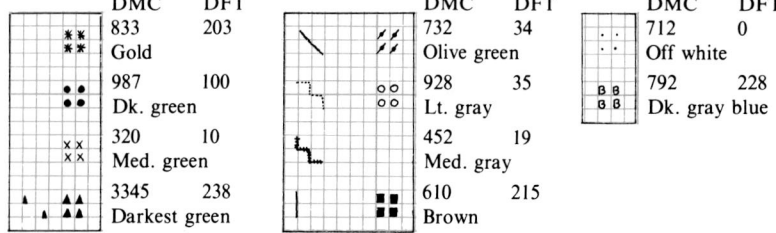

	DMC	DFT	
**	833	203	Gold
●●	987	100	Dk. green
xx	320	10	Med. green
▲▲	3345	238	Darkest green
∕∕	732	34	Olive green
○○	928	35	Lt. gray
	452	19	Med. gray
■■	610	215	Brown
∙∙	712	0	Off white
BB	792	228	Dk. gray blue

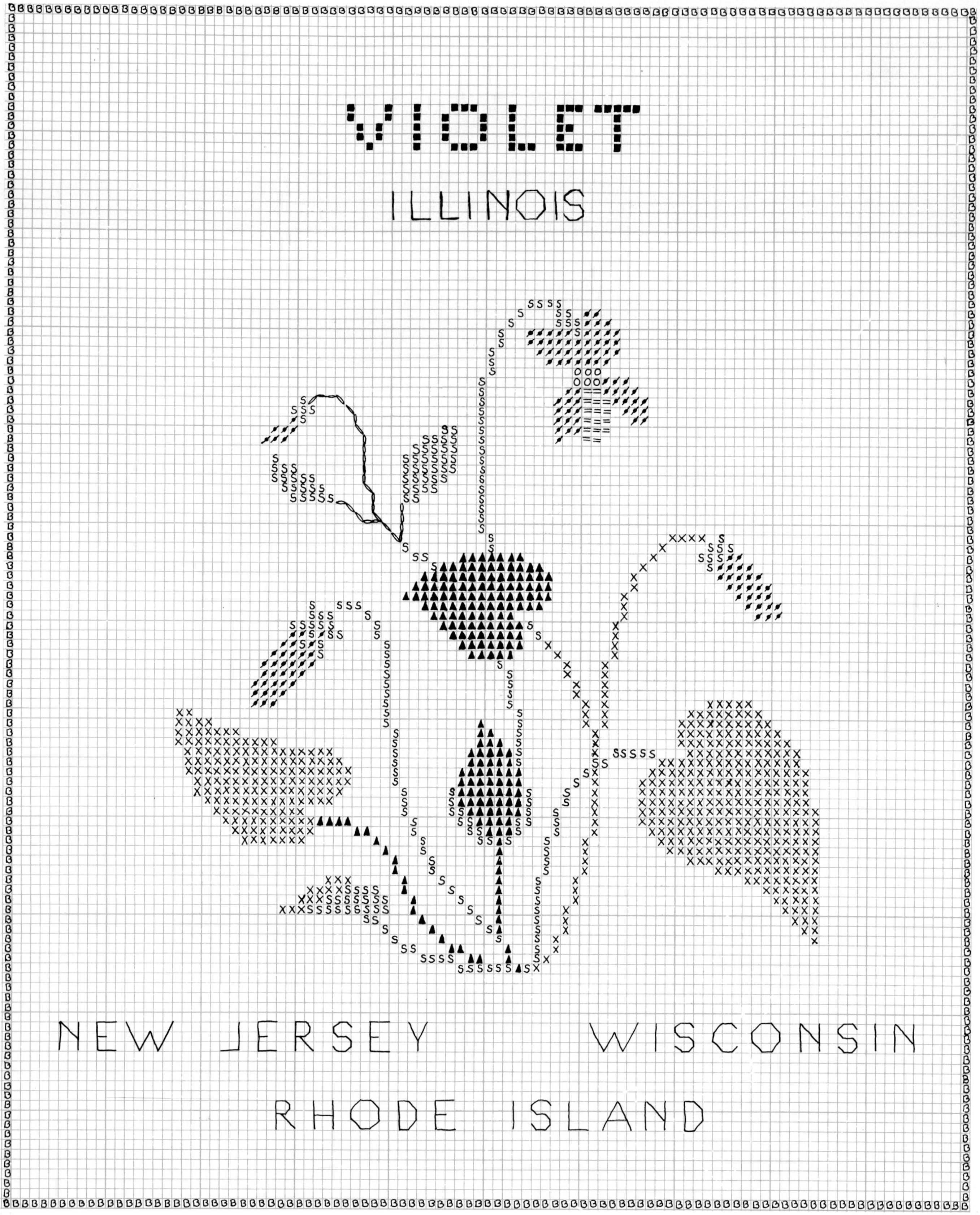

VIOLET
ILLINOIS

NEW JERSEY WISCONSIN
RHODE ISLAND

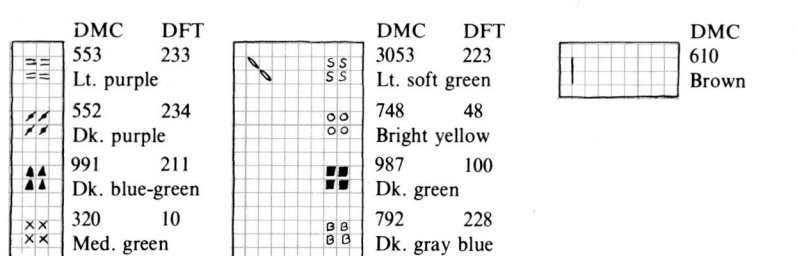

DMC	DFT
553	233
Lt. purple	
552	234
Dk. purple	
991	211
Dk. blue-green	
320	10
Med. green	

DMC	DFT
3053	223
Lt. soft green	
748	48
Bright yellow	
987	100
Dk. green	
792	228
Dk. gray blue	

DMC	DFT
610	215
Brown	

VIOLET
ILLINOIS

PEONY
INDIANA

DMC	DFT		DMC	DFT		DMC	DFT		DMC	DFT
776	69		3053	223		3685	411		792	228
Lt. pink			Lt. soft green			Med. burgundy			Dk. gray blue	
962	2		320	10		223	15		610	215
Med. dusty pink			Med. green			Grayish red			Brown	
961	37		987	100		832	6			
Med. pink			Dk. green			Dk. gold-green				
600	88		991	211						
Med. red			Dk. blue-green							

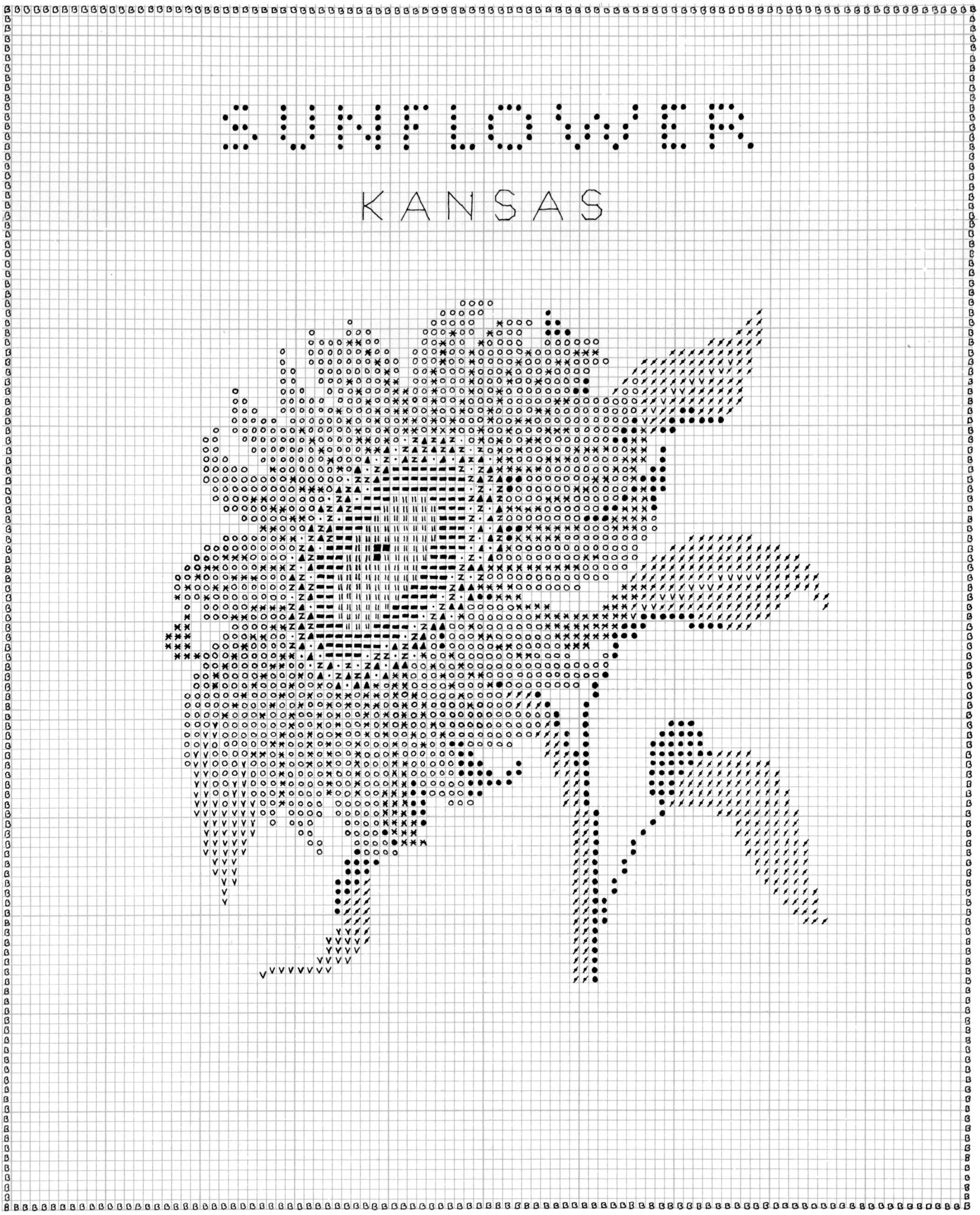

SUNFLOWER
KANSAS

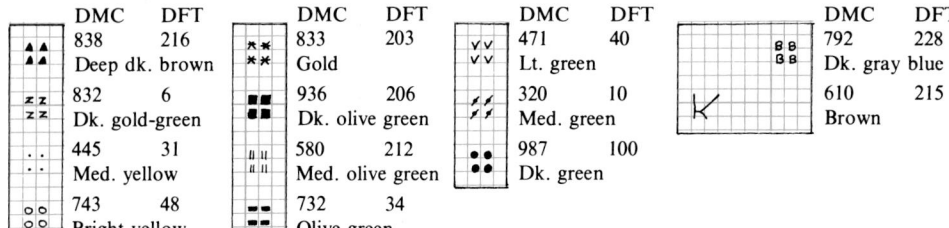

	DMC	DFT		DMC	DFT		DMC	DFT		DMC	DFT
▲▲	838	216	✱✱	833	203	ᵛᵛ	471	40	ᴮᴮ	792	228
	Deep dk. brown			Gold			Lt. green			Dk. gray blue	
ᶻᶻ	832	6	■■	936	206	∕∕	320	10	K	610	215
	Dk. gold-green			Dk. olive green			Med. green			Brown	
··	445	31	‖‖	580	212	••	987	100			
	Med. yellow			Med. olive green			Dk. green				
○○	743	48	━━	732	34						
	Bright yellow			Olive green							

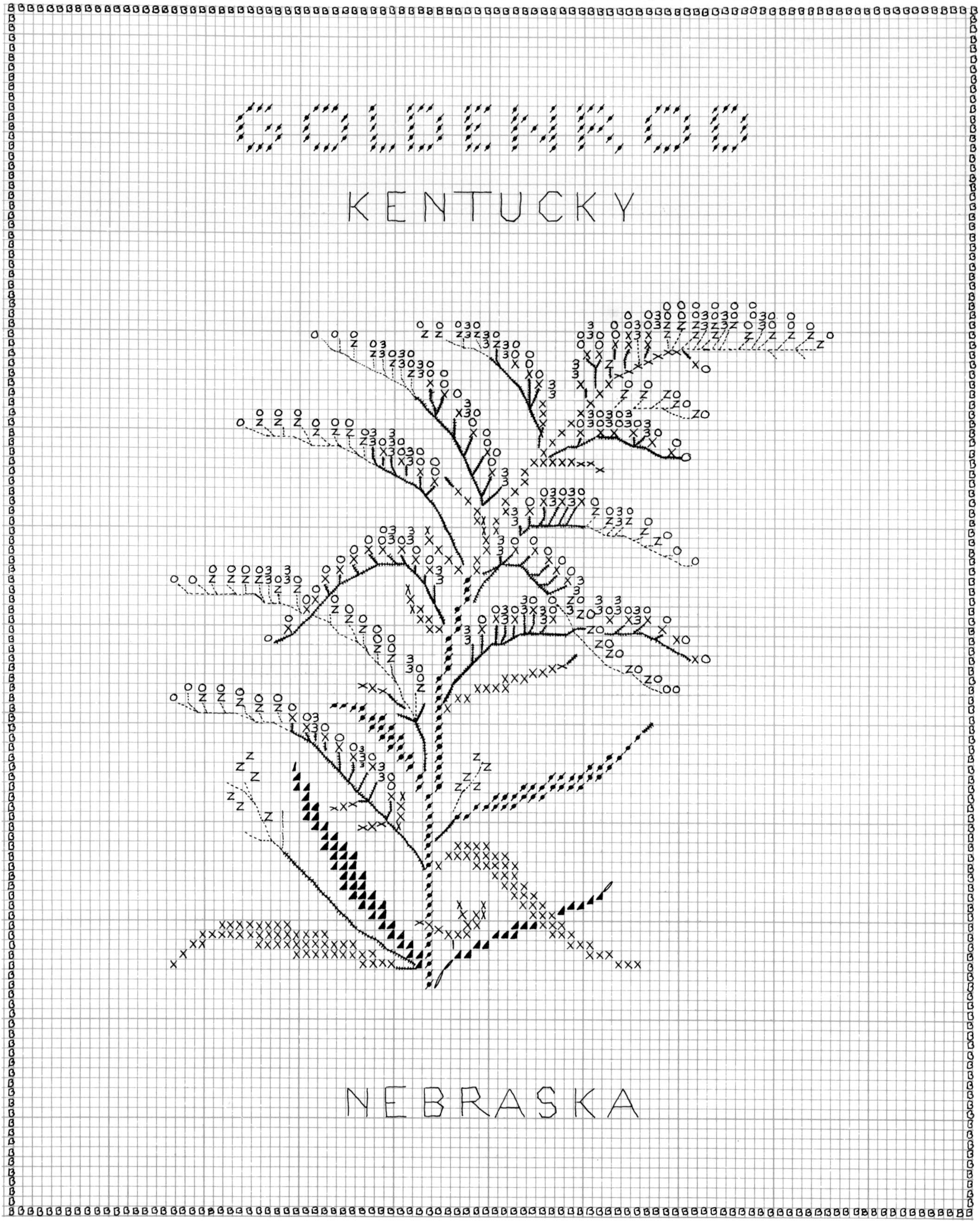

GOLDENROD
KENTUCKY

NEBRASKA

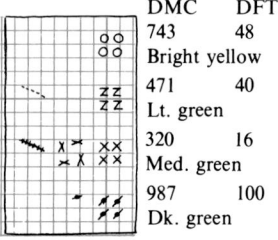
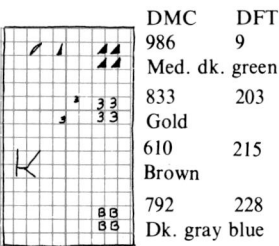

	DMC	DFT	
oo / oo	743	48	Bright yellow
zz / zz	471	40	Lt. green
xx / xx	320	16	Med. green
	987	100	Dk. green

	DMC	DFT	
◢◢ / ◢◢	986	9	Med. dk. green
33 / 33	833	203	Gold
K	610	215	Brown
BB / BB	792	228	Dk. gray blue

GOLDENROD
KENTUCKY

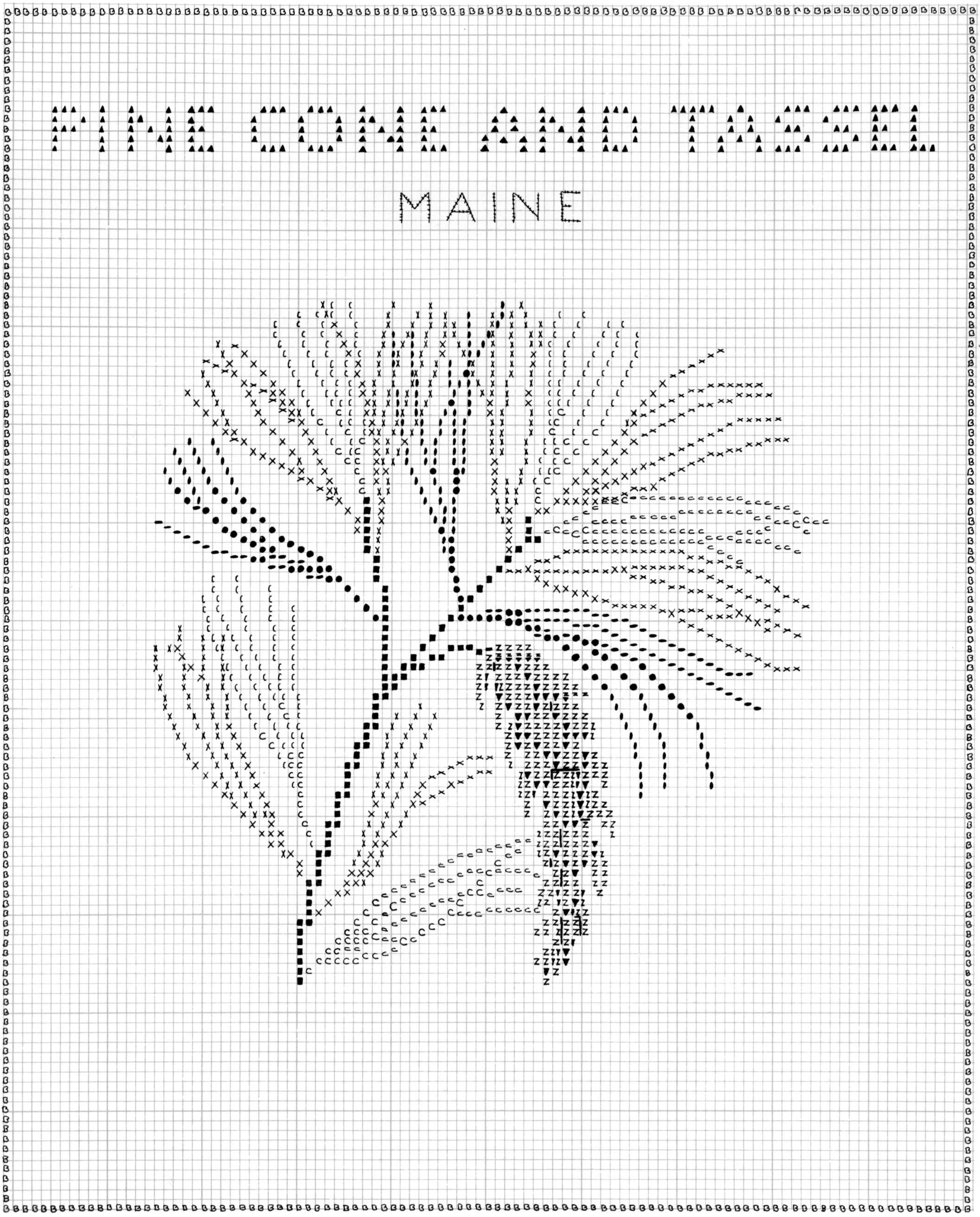

PINE CONE AND TASSEL
MAINE

DMC	DFT	
300	214	Redish brown
781	213	Redish tan
368	224	Dk. soft green
910	8	Bright green
991	211	Dk. blue green
987	100	Dk. green
838	216	Deep dk. brown
610	215	Brown
792	228	Dk. gray blue

PINE CONE AND TASSEL
MAINE

BLACK-EYED SUSAN
MARYLAND

DMC	DFT		DMC	DFT		DMC	DFT
987	100		838	216		832	6
Dk. green			Deep dk. brown			Dk. gold-green	
3345	238		743	48		792	228
Darkest green			Bright yellow			Dk. gray blue	
320	10		610	215			
Med. green			Brown				
3053	223						
Lt. soft green							

BLACK-EYED SUSAN

MARYLAND

ARBUTUS
MASSACHUSETTS

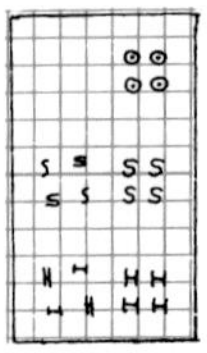

DMC	DFT	
743	48	Bright yellow
776	69	Lt. pink
3354	3	Lt. dusty pink

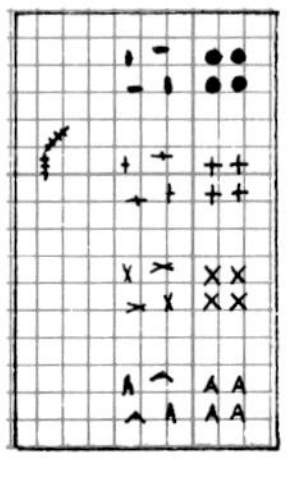

DMC	DFT	
3345	238	Darkest green
987	100	Dk. green
320	10	Med. green
3053	223	Lt. soft green

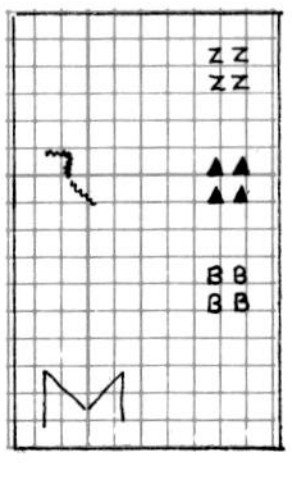

DMC	DFT	
781	213	Redish tan
300	214	Redish brown
792	228	Dk. gray blue
610	215	Brown

ARBUTUS
MASSACHUSETTS

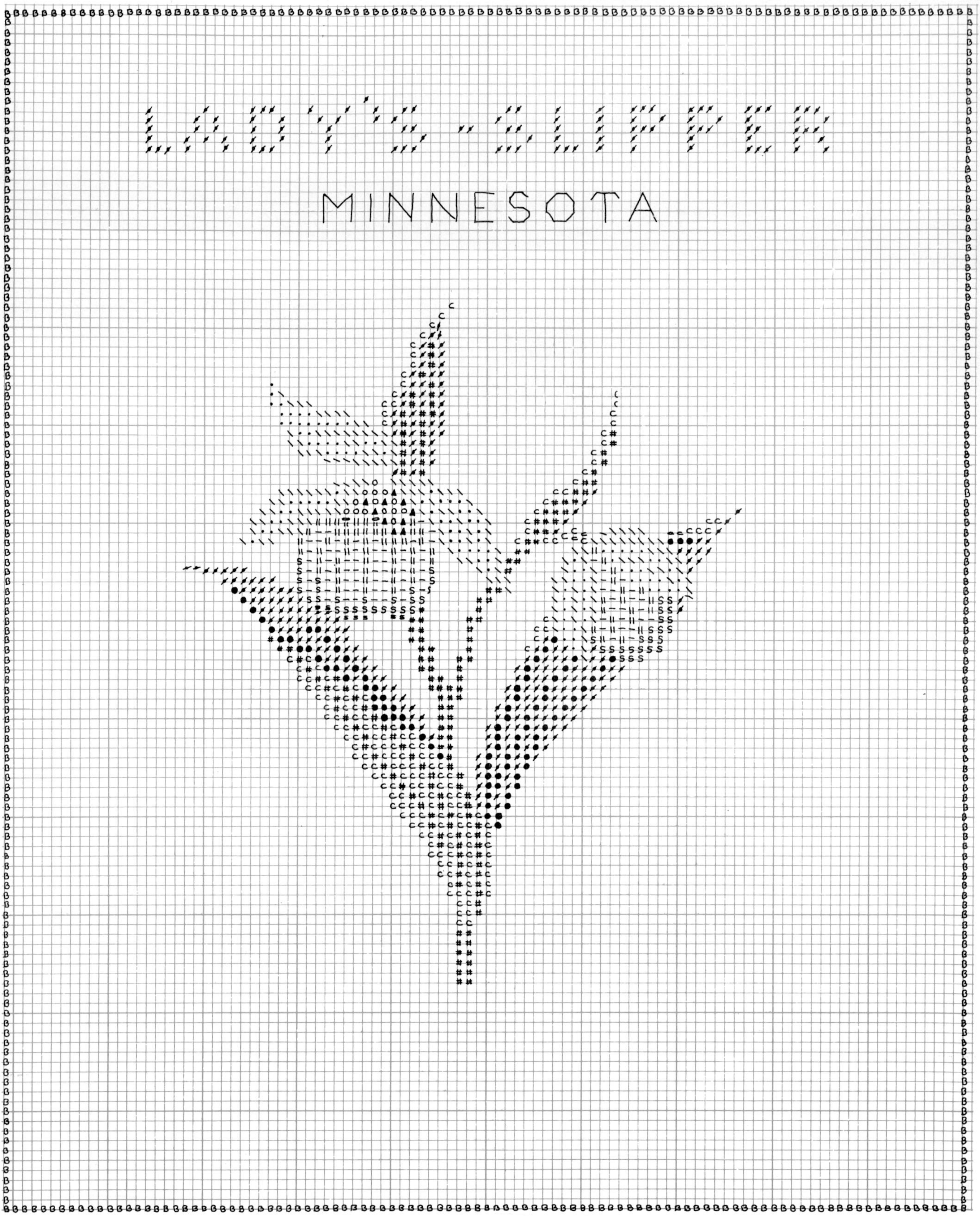

LADY'S-SLIPPER
MINNESOTA

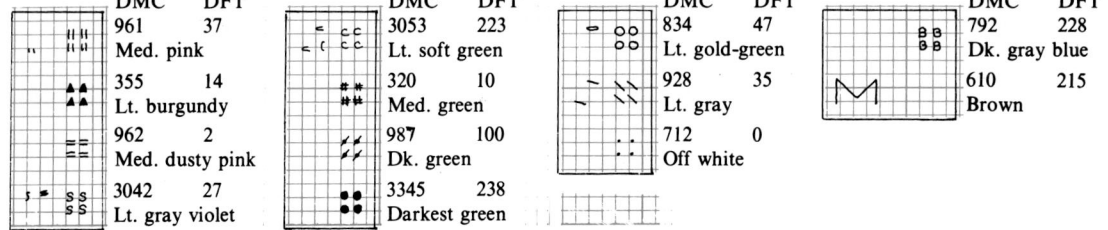

DMC	DFT		DMC	DFT		DMC	DFT		DMC	DFT
961	37		3053	223		834	47		792	228
Med. pink			Lt. soft green			Lt. gold-green			Dk. gray blue	
355	14		320	10		928	35		610	215
Lt. burgundy			Med. green			Lt. gray			Brown	
962	2		987	100		712	0			
Med. dusty pink			Dk. green			Off white				
3042	27		3345	238						
Lt. gray violet			Darkest green							

LADY'S-SLIPPER
MINNESOTA

HAWTHORN
MISSOURI

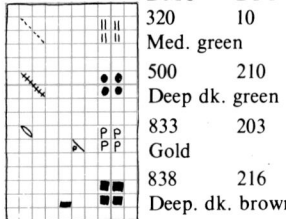

DMC	DFT		DMC	DFT		DMC	DFT		DMC	DFT
320	10		3345	238		902	4		987	100
Med. green			Darkest green			Dk. burgundy			Dk. green	
500	210		986	9		3685	411		792	228
Deep dk. green			Med. dk. green			Med. burgundy			Dk. gray blue	
833	203		3053	223		600	88		610	215
Gold			Lt. soft green			Med. red			Brown	
838	216		734	26		760	12			
Deep. dk. brown			Med. gold-green			Lt. salmon				

BITTERROOT
MONTANA

DMC	DFT	
677	225	Lt. gold
3354	3	Lt. dusty pink
776	69	Lt. pink
832	6	Dk. gold green

DMC	DFT	
3053	223	Lt. soft green
320	10	Med. green
987	100	Dk. green

DMC	DFT	
223	15	Grayish red
838	216	Deep dk. brown
792	228	Dk. gray blue
610	215	Brown

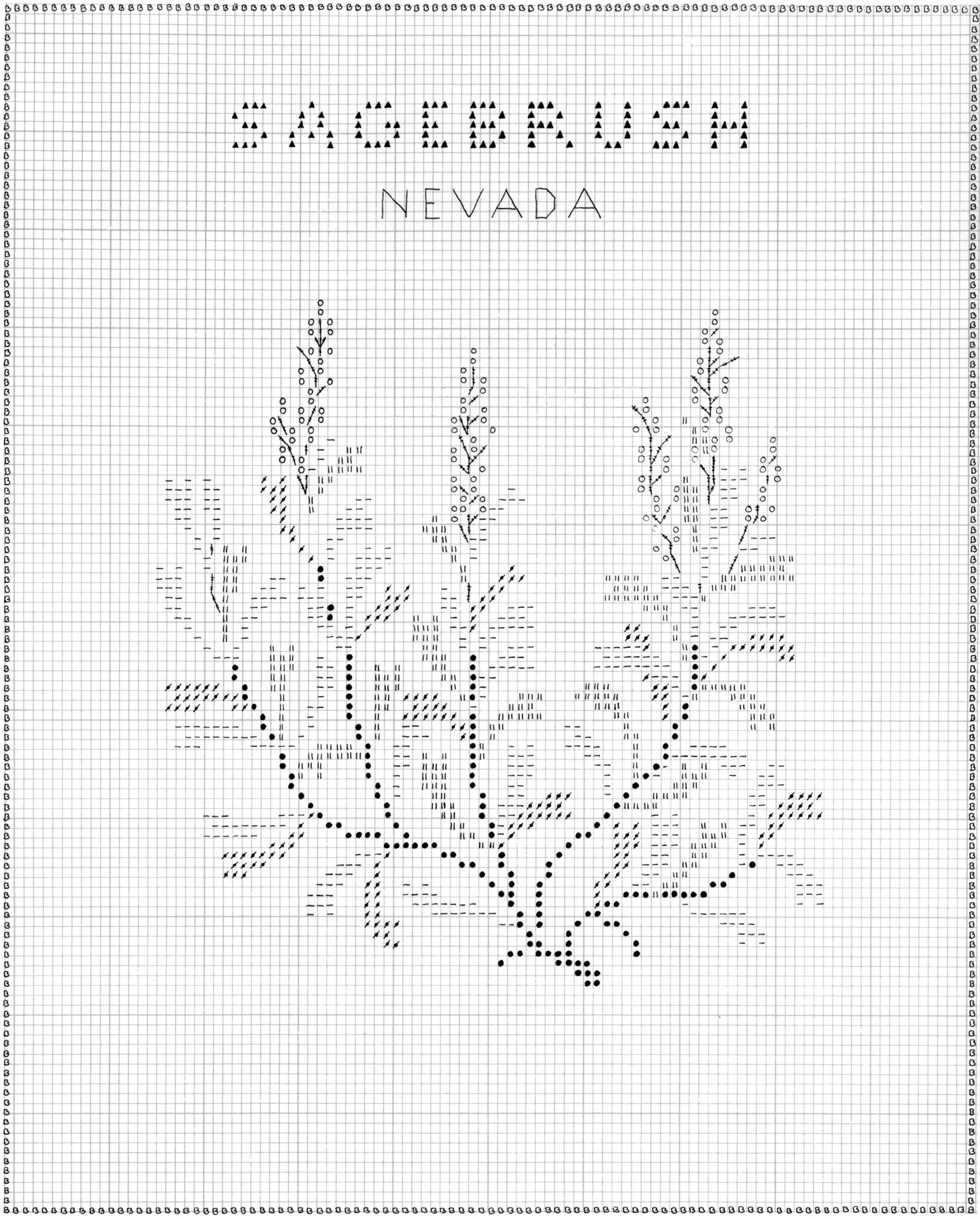

SAGEBRUSH
NEVADA

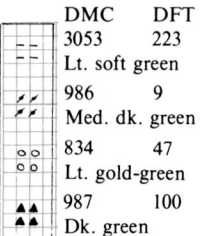

	DMC	DFT	
-- --	3053	223	Lt. soft green
//	986	9	Med. dk. green
o o	834	47	Lt. gold-green
▲▲	987	100	Dk. green

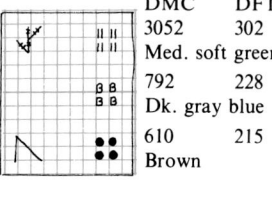

	DMC	DFT	
↓ ‖ ‖	3052	302	Med. soft green
B B	792	228	Dk. gray blue
N ●●	610	215	Brown

YUCCA
NEW MEXICO

	DMC	DFT		DMC	DFT		DMC	DFT
▲▲	316	235	‖ ‖	734	26	z z	368	224
	Pink violet			Med. gold-green			Dk. soft green	
oo	950	25	∕∕	3052	302	■■	987	100
	Flesh pink			Med. soft green			Dk. green	
..	712	0	××	3053	223	BB	792	228
	Off white			Lt. soft green			Dk. gray blue	
--	677	225	●●	986	9	∧	610	215
	Lt. gold			Med. dk. green			Brown	

SAGEBRUSH
NEVADA

YUCCA
NEW MEXICO

	DMC	DFT		DMC	DFT		DMC	DFT
▲▲	316	235	‖‖	734	26	zz	368	224
▲▲	Pink violet		‖‖	Med. gold-green		zz	Dk. soft green	
oo	950	25	⁄⁄	3052	302	■■	987	100
oo	Flesh pink		⁄⁄	Med. soft green		■■	Dk. green	
··	712	0	xx	3053	223	BB	792	228
··	Off white		xx	Lt. soft green		BB	Dk. gray blue	
−−	677	225	●●	986	9	◣	610	215
−−	Lt. gold		●●	Med. dk. green			Brown	

WILD ROSE

NEW YORK

IOWA   NORTH DAKOTA

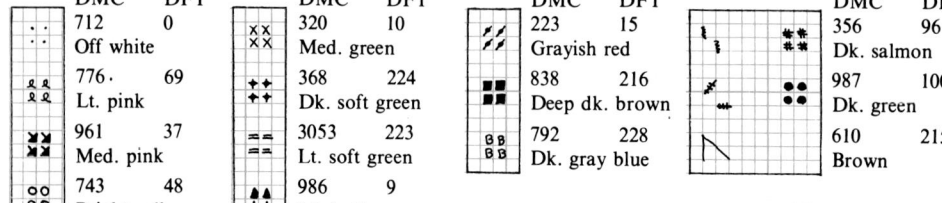

DMC	DFT		DMC	DFT		DMC	DFT		DMC	DFT
712	0		320	10		223	15		356	96
Off white			Med. green			Grayish red			Dk. salmon	
776	69		368	224		838	216		987	100
Lt. pink			Dk. soft green			Deep dk. brown			Dk. green	
961	37		3053	223		792	228		610	215
Med. pink			Lt. soft green			Dk. gray blue			Brown	
743	48		986	9						
Bright yellow			Med. dk. green							

WILD ROSE
NEW YORK

NORTH CAROLINA

VIRGINIA

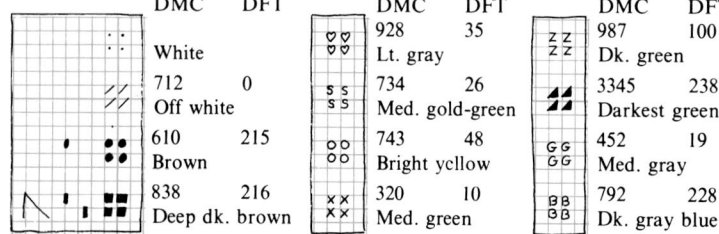

	DMC	DFT		DMC	DFT		DMC	DFT
			♡♡	928	35	ZZ	987	100
	White			Lt. gray		ZZ	Dk. green	
//	712	0	SS	734	26	▲▲	3345	238
	Off white		SS	Med. gold-green		▲▲	Darkest green	
••	610	215	OO	743	48	GG	452	19
	Brown		OO	Bright yellow		GG	Med. gray	
■■	838	216	XX	320	10	BB	792	228
	Deep dk. brown			Med. green		BB	Dk. gray blue	

FLOWERING DOGWOOD

VIRGINIA

CARNATION
OHIO

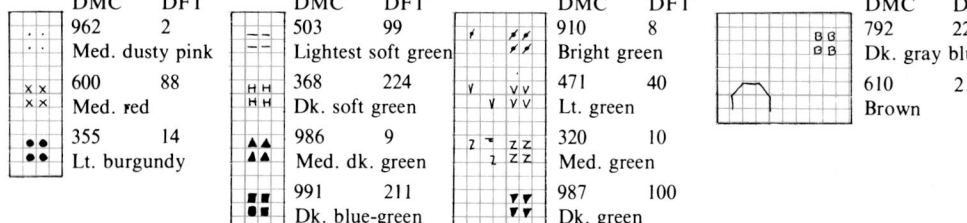

DMC	DFT		DMC	DFT		DMC	DFT		DMC	DFT
962	2		503	99		910	8		792	228
Med. dusty pink			Lightest soft green			Bright green			Dk. gray blue	
600	88		368	224		471	40		610	215
Med. red			Dk. soft green			Lt. green			Brown	
355	14		986	9		320	10			
Lt. burgundy			Med. dk. green			Med. green				
			991	211		987	100			
			Dk. blue-green			Dk. green				

	DMC	DFT
Lt. gray	928	35
Olive green	732	34
Off white	712	0
Med. gray	452	19
Med. green	320	10
Lt. green	471	40
Darkest green	3345	238
Dk. green	987	100
Dk. gray blue	792	228
Brown	610	215

OREGON GRAPE
OREGON

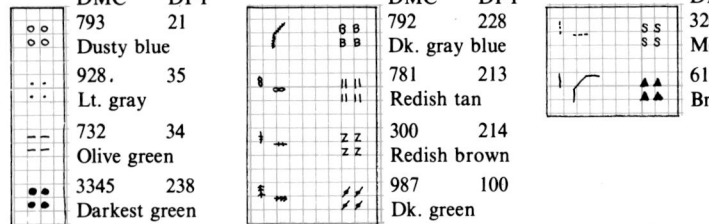

	DMC	DFT			DMC	DFT			DMC	DFT
o o	793	21		B B	792	228		s s	320	10
	Dusty blue				Dk. gray blue				Med. green	
. .	928	35		o	781	213		▲ ▲	610	215
	Lt. gray				Redish tan				Brown	
— —	732	34		z z	300	214				
	Olive green				Redish brown					
● ●	3345	238			987	100				
	Darkest green				Dk. green					

OREGON GRAPE
OREGON

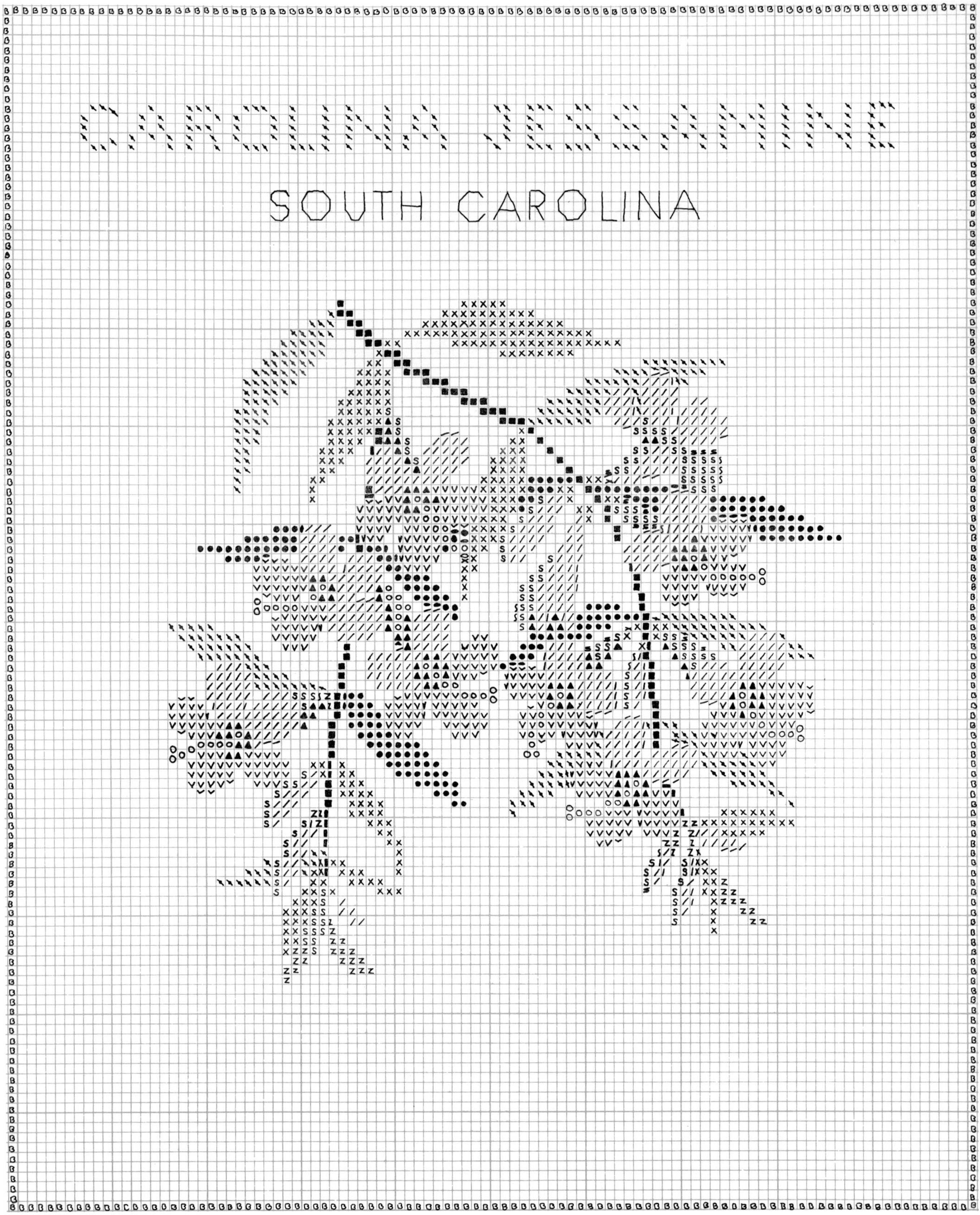

CAROLINA JESSAMINE
SOUTH CAROLINA

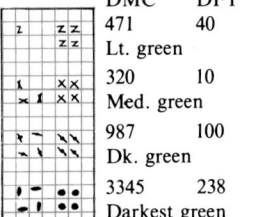

	DMC	DFT
z	471	40
	Lt. green	
x	320	10
	Med. green	
	987	100
	Dk. green	
•	3345	238
	Darkest green	

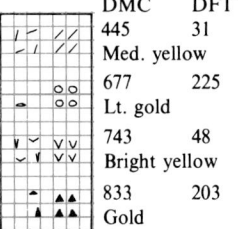

	DMC	DFT
/	445	31
	Med. yellow	
o	677	225
	Lt. gold	
v	743	48
	Bright yellow	
▲	833	203
	Gold	

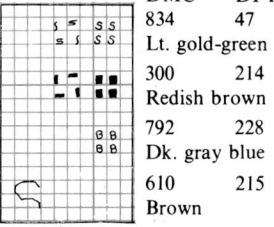

	DMC	DFT
s	834	47
	Lt. gold-green	
■	300	214
	Redish brown	
B	792	228
	Dk. gray blue	
⌒	610	215
	Brown	

CAROLINA JESSAMINE
SOUTH CAROLINA

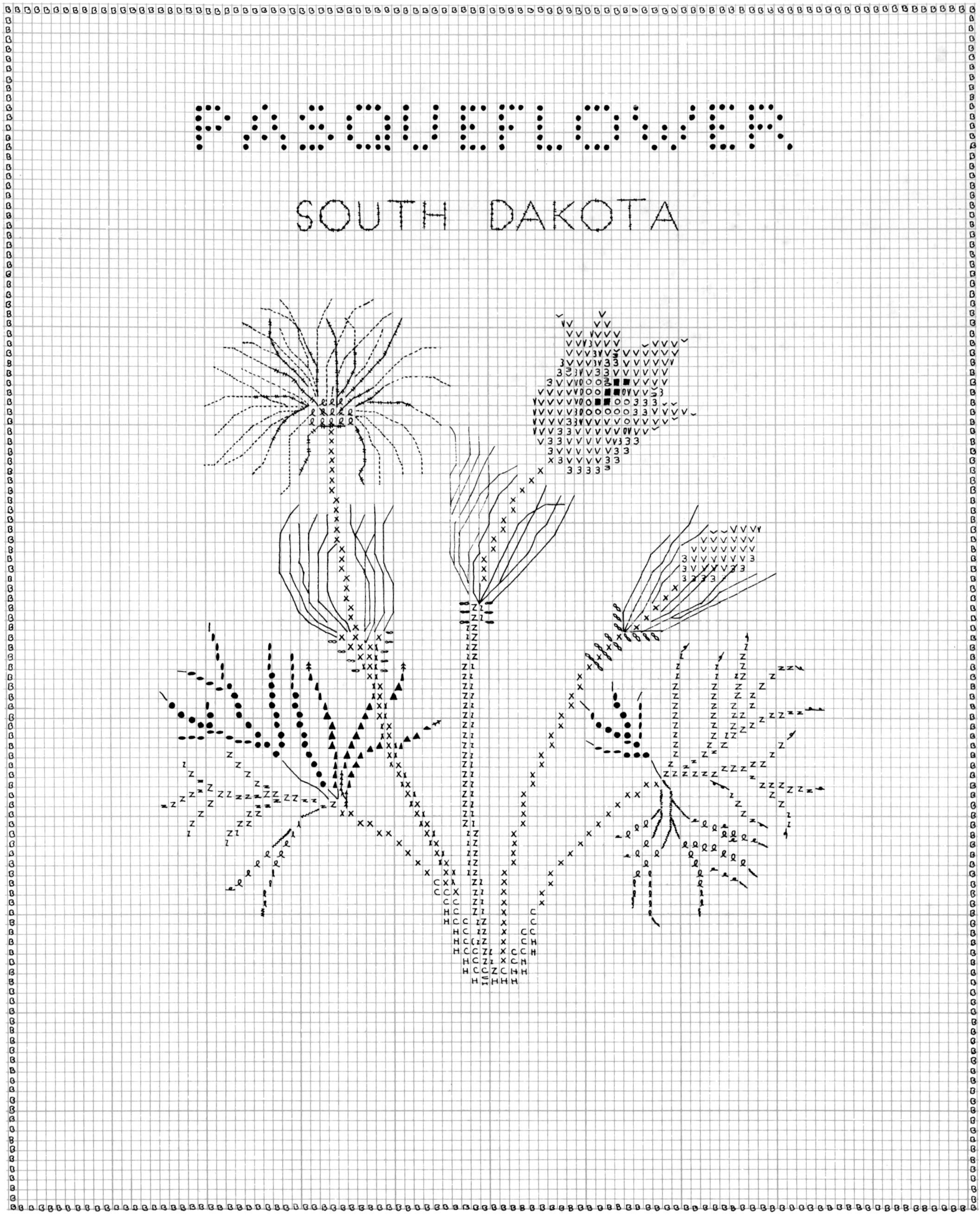

PASQUEFLOWER
SOUTH DAKOTA

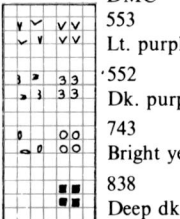

	DMC	DFT
Lt. purple	553	233
Dk. purple	552	234
Bright yellow	743	48
Deep dk. brown	838	216

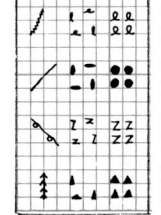

	DMC	DFT
Lt. soft green	3053	223
Lt. gold	677	225
Dk. gray blue	792	228

	DMC	DFT
Lt. green	471	40
Dk. green	987	100
Med. green	320	10
Darkest green	3345	238

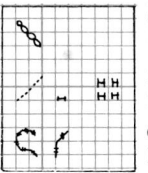

	DMC	DFT
Lt. gray	928	35
Dk. beige	3032	222
Brown	610	215

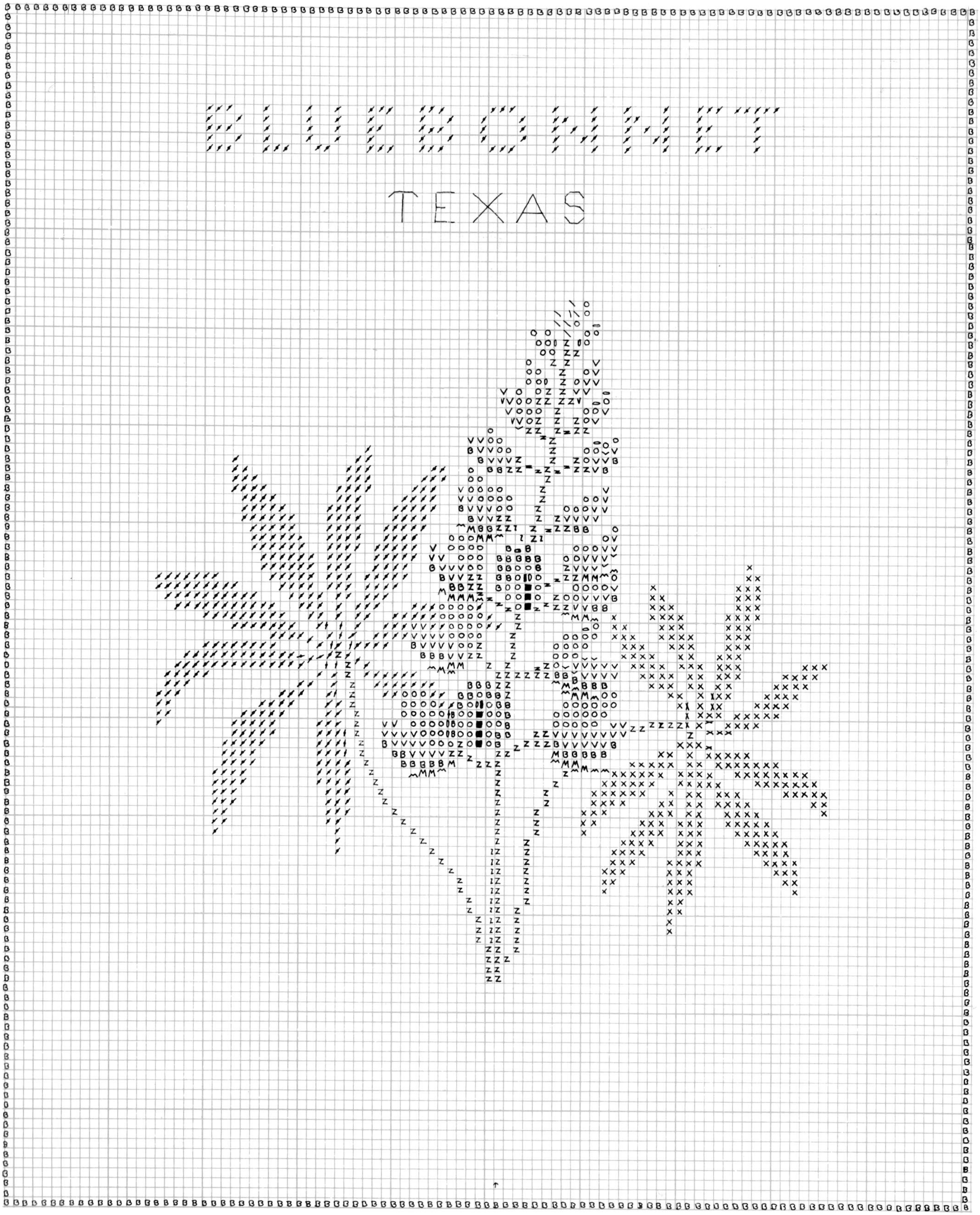

BLUEBONNET
TEXAS

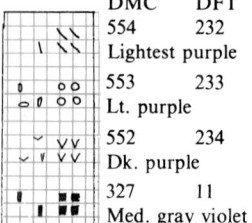
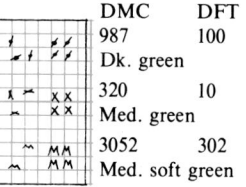
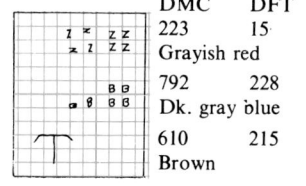

DMC	DFT	
554	232	Lightest purple
553	233	Lt. purple
552	234	Dk. purple
327	11	Med. gray violet
987	100	Dk. green
320	10	Med. green
3052	302	Med. soft green
223	15	Grayish red
792	228	Dk. gray blue
610	215	Brown

BLUEBONNET
TEXAS

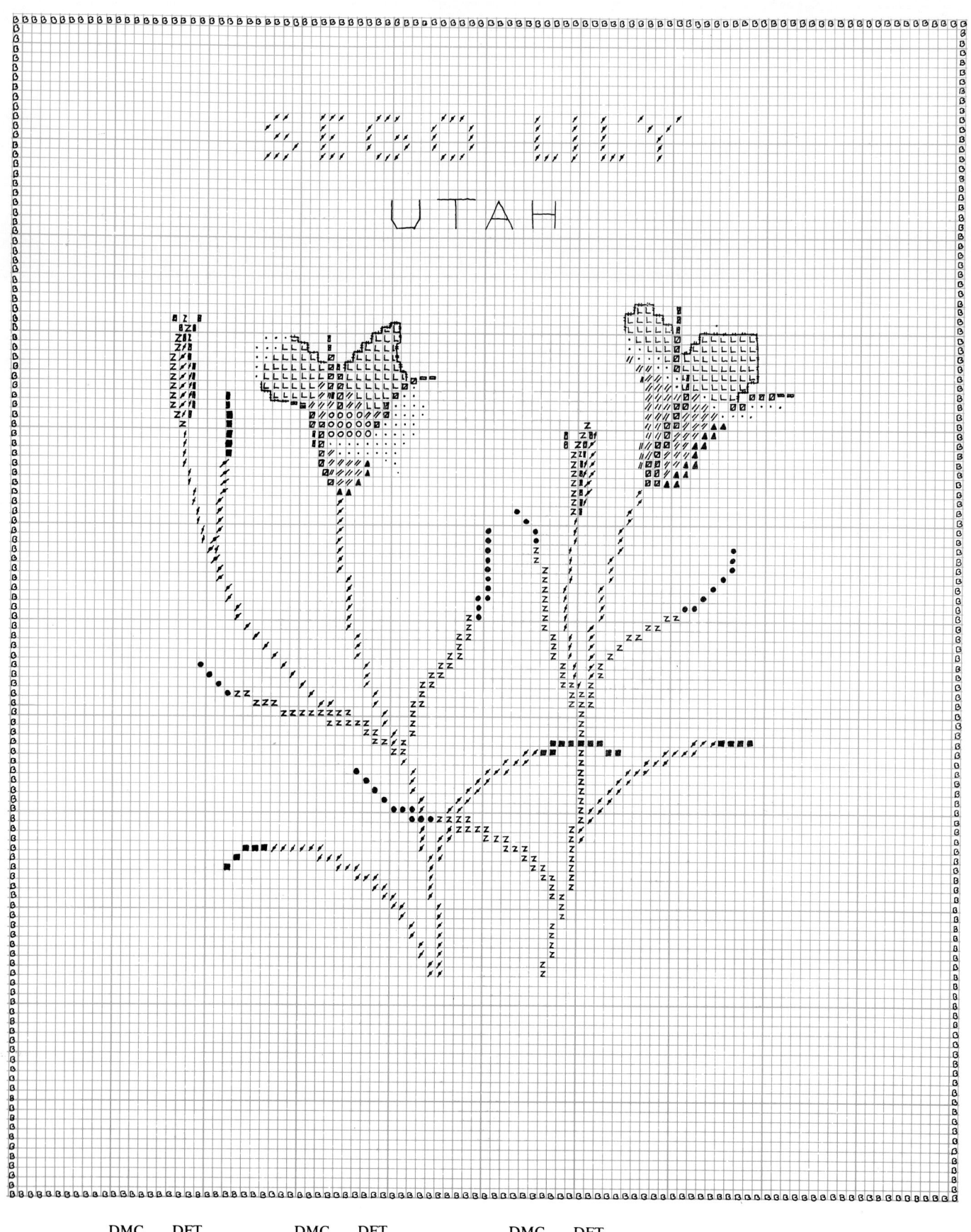

SEGO LILY
UTAH

RED CLOVER
VERMONT

DMC	DFT	
3350	205	Dk. pink
962	2	Med. dusty pink
452	19	Med. gray

DMC	DFT	
986	9	Med. dk. green
320	10	Med. green
3053	223	Lt. soft green
987	100	Dk. green

DMC	DFT	
792	228	Dk. gray blue
610	215	Brown

WASHINGTON

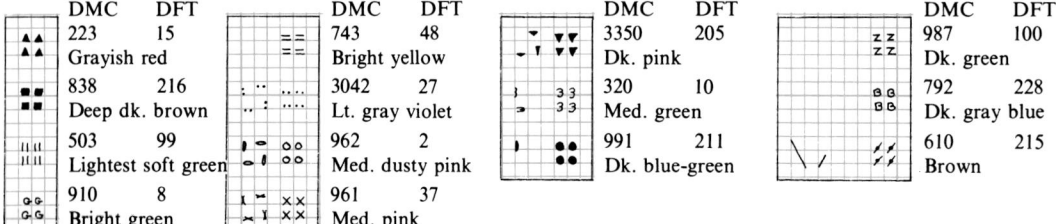

DMC	DFT		DMC	DFT		DMC	DFT		DMC	DFT
223	15		743	48		3350	205		987	100
Grayish red			Bright yellow			Dk. pink			Dk. green	
838	216		3042	27		320	10		792	228
Deep dk. brown			Lt. gray violet			Med. green			Dk. gray blue	
503	99		962	2		991	211		610	215
Lightest soft green			Med. dusty pink			Dk. blue-green			Brown	
910	8		961	37						
Bright green			Med. pink							

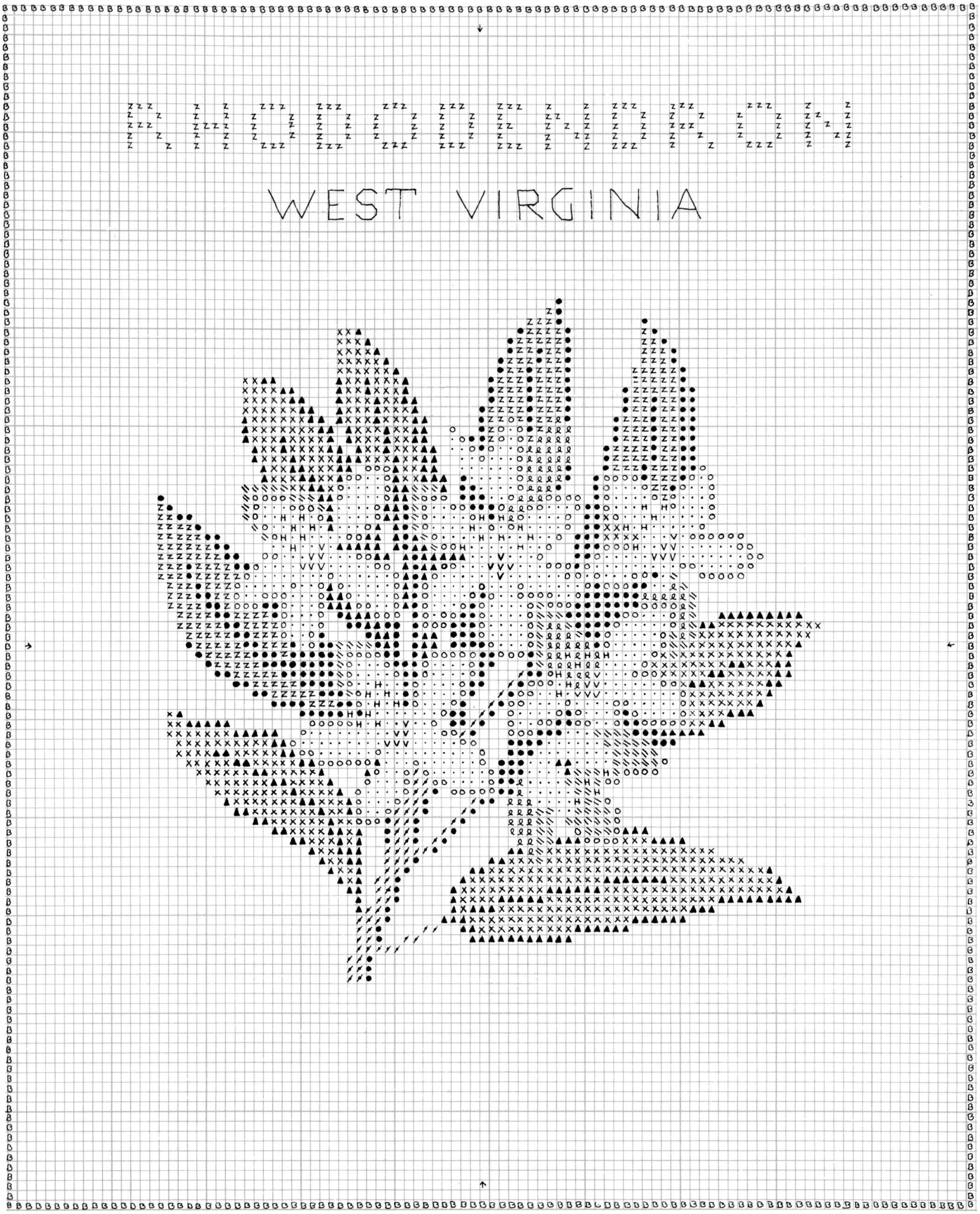

WEST VIRGINIA

	DMC	DFT		DMC	DFT		DMC	DFT		DMC	DFT
∘∘	225		HH	734	26	zz	987	100	BB	792	228
	Soft pink			Med. gold-green			Dk. green			Dk. gray blue	
ℓℓ	928	35	vv	3053	223	••	500	210	∨	610	215
	Lt. gray			Lt. soft green			Deep dk. green			Brown	
··	712	0	//	580	212	▲▲	3345	238			
	Off white			Med. olive green			Darkest green				
\\	3042	27	xx	320	10						
	Lt. gray violet			Med. green							

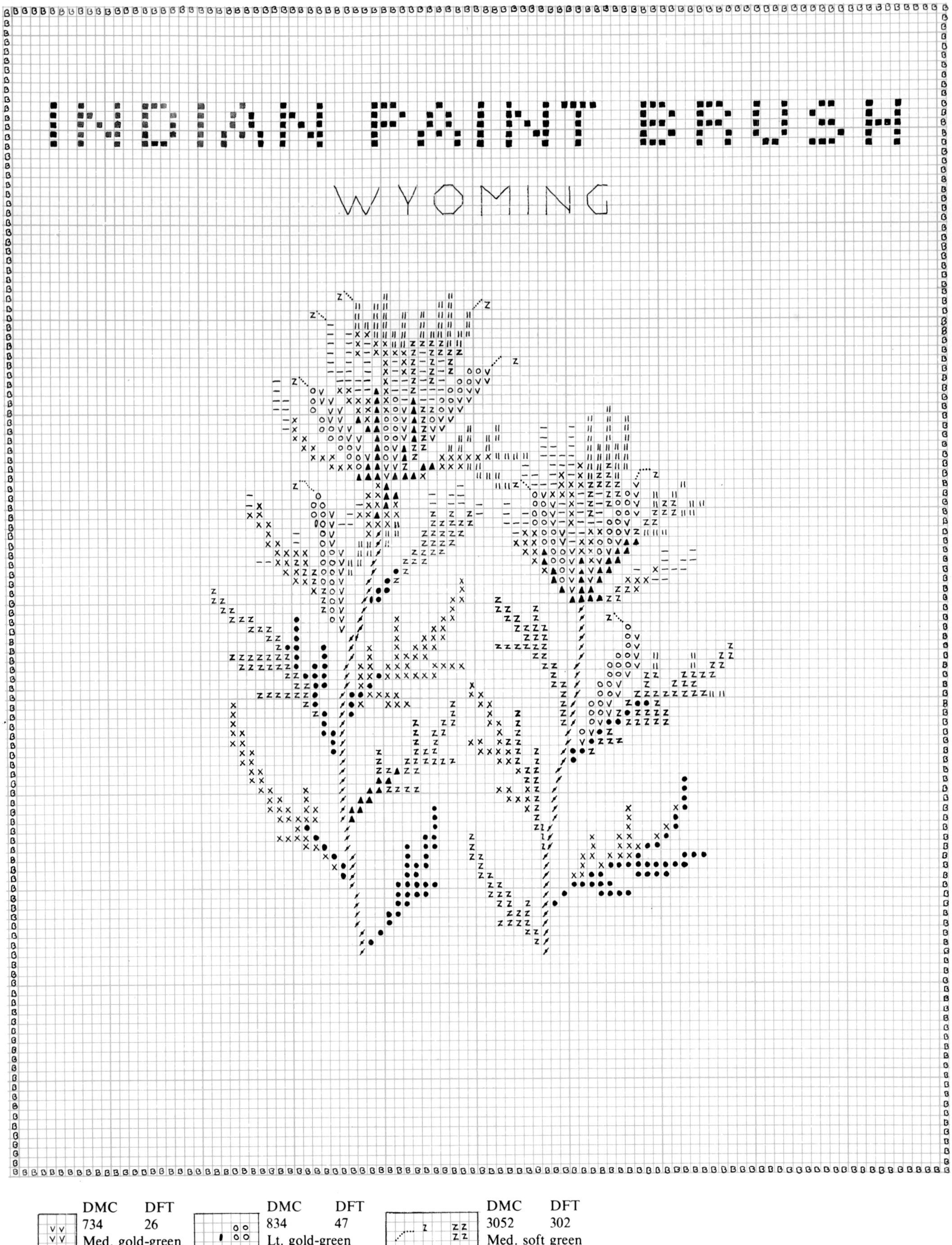

INDIAN PAINT BRUSH
WYOMING

	DMC	DFT			DMC	DFT			DMC	DFT
v v	734	26		o o	834	47		z z	3052	302
	Med. gold-green				Lt. gold-green				Med. soft green	
– –	922	93		/ /	223	15		■ ■	987	100
	Lt. orange				Grayish red				Dk. green	
‖ ‖	921	95		x x	3053	223		B B	792	228
	Med. orange				Lt. soft green				Dk. gray blue	
▲ ▲	732	34		• •	3345	238		\ \	610	215
	Olive green				Darkest green				Brown	

INDIAN PAINT BRUSH
WYOMING

SUPPLIERS

These suppliers sell wholesale only. They will be happy to supply you with a list of retail outlets in your area that carry cross-stitch materials.

Counted Thread Society of America
3305 South Newport Street
Denver, CO 80222

Cross Stitch Country, Inc.
P.O.B. 825
Pawleys Island, S.C. 29585
(Supplier of Danish Flower Thread)

Joan Toggitt
246 Fifth Avenue
New York, NY 10001

INDEX

American Beauty Rose (District of Columbia) 30
Apple Blossom (Arkansas, Michigan) 20
Arbutus (Massachusetts) 54
Bitterroot (Montana) 60
Black-Eyed Susan (Maryland) 52
Bluebonnet (Texas) 84
California Poppy (California) 22
Camellia (Alabama) 14
Carnation (Ohio) 72
Carolina Jessamine (South Carolina) 78
Cherokee Rose (Georgia) 34
Columbine (Colorado) 24
Flowering Dogwood (Virginia, North Carolina) 70
Forget-Me-Not (Alaska) 16
Goldenrod (Kentucky, Nebraska) 46
Hawthorn (Missouri) 58
Indian Paint Brush (Wyoming) 94
Iris (Tennessee) 82
Lady's Slipper (Minnesota) 56
Lilac (New Hampshire) 64
Magnolia (Louisiana, Mississippi) 48
Mistletoe (Oklahoma) 74
Mountain Laurel (Connecticut, Pennsylvania) 26
Orange Blossom (Florida) 32
Oregon Grape (Oregon) 76
Pasqueflower (South Dakota) 80
Peach Blossom (Delaware) 28
Peony (Indiana) 42
Pine Cone and Tassel (Maine) 50
Pink Rhododendron (Washington) 90
Red Clover (Vermont) 88
Red Hibiscus (Hawaii) 36
Rhododendron (West Virginia) 92
Sagebrush (Nevada) 62
Saguaro (Arizona) 18
Sego Lily (Utah) 86
Sunflower (Kansas) 44
Syringa (Idaho) 38
Violet (Illinois, Wisconsin, Rhode Island, New Jersey) 40
Wild Rose (New York, North Dakota, Iowa) 68
Yucca (New Mexico) 66